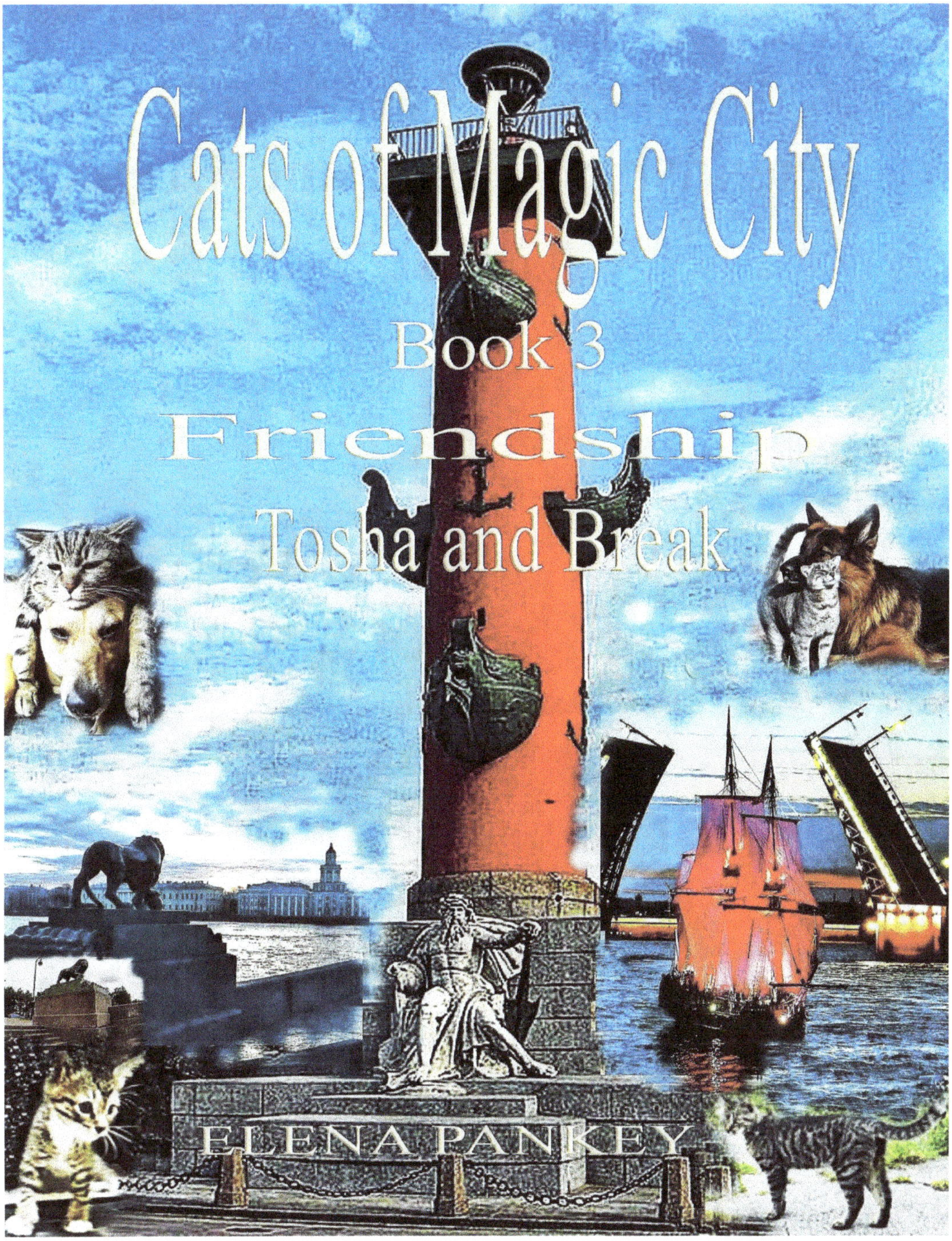
Cats of Magic City
Book 3
Friendship
Tosha and Break
ELENA PANKEY

978-1-950311-81-1

Cats of Magic City

Book 3

Friendship. Tosha and Break

Elena Pankey

AllRightsReserved@2020ElenaPankey

No copyright infringement is int

Contents

About Trilogy	4
Solution	6
Puppy Break	9
Cat and Dog	11
Respect	14
Games	17
Winter	18
Tosha's Hobby	20
Be useful	21
Family vacation	23
Vacation	24
Dog School	25
Circumstances	27
Tosha's Dream	29
Enjoy each day	31
Our pets	31
Author	33
All rights reserved	34

About Trilogy

These are three fascinating, colorful books for children. Each of them is a continuation of the previous one. All three of them are fascinating and colorful books for children of any age.

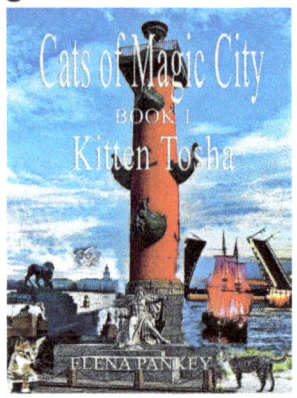  

Book 1 "Cats of Magic City. Kitten Tosha." It is about the kittens of the magical, Russian city of St. Petersburg. It gives the short information about the embankments of St. Petersburg, where cats live and have fun. This is a story about the birth of a kitten Tosha, about his friends who lived under the bridges of a magical city on the Neva River. Cats strive to be like their distant relatives - lions. Many sculptures of Lions are everywhere on the embankments. Cat Vasily told the legends of the sphinx and griffins.

Book 2 "Cats of Magic City. Dreams and Realities of Cat Tosha" tells about Tosha's flights from the balcony, his trip to the Black Sea, his nightly adventures and battles with the local cats on the Black sea. Tosha was sure that he was the highest being, and sought to subjugate all who lived nearby. When he happened to visit Gelendzik, he met local cats there and fought for his life. Then, cat Tosha reevaluated his St. Petersburg sybaritic life. He began to cherish everything that he had before his trip to the South.

Book 3 "Cat's of Magic City. Friendship. Tosha and Break" tells about the friendship of the cat Tosha and new puppy Break. The books contain many color drawings and funny stories of the Author's cat Tosha. It has instructive facts of the life of cats. Entertaining information about the character and habits of the beloved pets will allow parents to share a pleasant time with their children. Reading books and joint pastime will make family life more joyful.

***

In the meantime, let's learn one wisdom that will help to understand the difference between a cat and a dog. "If the tail of the cat is at rest, then your cat is calm. Suddenly he swings his tail, which means he is nervous. In the dogs the opposite is true. The tail plays a different role. And therefore, so often the cats do not understand the dog's body language. But I'll tell you a secret; there is no stronger cat-dog friendship. If people were friends like some cat and dog, everyone around the world would only live in peace".

Solution

Once upon a time, cat Tosha was born in the magical city of St. Petersburg. The good girl Lila took him to her apartment and raised him. Tosha never left it, and only from time to time flew after the birds from the balcony, which was on the fourth floor. He just dreamed about some active social life. Then, the good girl Lila and her parents took Tosha to a vacation. After several days in a very uncomfortable train, they visited grandmother house in Gelendzhik on the Black Sea. There Tosha met some bold bully, local bandit cats. He fought fiercely for his life.

After defeating a local Gelendzhik cat, Tosha believed that now he was a real hero. He felt like he was an unrecognized genius. Tosha was sure that the whole world should already have known about his adventures. A trip to the southern resort and a battle in the grandmother's garden with local cats taught Tosha a lot. But the main quality of all people, the modesty was not increased in him yet. But the memory of these incredible events for a long time did not let the cat Tosha sleep peacefully.

When he returned back home to St. Petersburg, he was expecting some respectful signs of attention. "Well, everyone could at least read about it somewhere or see on TV,"- thought Tosha. Sometimes, he reminded his beloved artist Valery, that the mistress of the house, mother Alena, refused to eat the fresh sparrows, which he so successfully caught on the ledge and brought for her. Then, he recalled that the good girl Lila often came back from her school too late, and missed his specific feeding time. And the most importantly, the cat believed that the family took him far south, against his own free will, without asking him.

However, before all of that, Tosha often dreamed about the high life and longed for some adventures. Details about the fascinating life of the cat Tosha read in the Book 1 and Book 2 of this trilogy.

Finally, the owners realized why Tosha has his endless "meows". He clearly needed to take care of someone. He had few relatives who loved him, but they spent most of the day at work and at school. Tosha dreamed of having a loyal friend with whom he would share the whole day together. Tosha even once thought that he might be would be able to share his fish with a friend.

He saw from the window of his house that other cats had their own pets - dogs. So Tosha started to dream about a puppy who would become his faithful friend and participant in the games. Tosha was sure that he could take care of the puppy.

Every day the cat Tosha looked more and more unhappy. It was the time to help him. Then having discussed everything, the family found an original way to do this. They bought a little German shepherd puppy Break. This is where the new, happiest page of Tosha's life began.

Puppy Break

When the puppy arrived from Germany, the artist Valery and the girl Lila went to the rail station to meet new family member. Mistress of the house, mother Alena with her cat Tosha was waiting for them at home, in a warm and comfortable apartment.

The puppy was marvelous and cute. In his passport, that came with him, his name "Break" was written in black and white. Break looked like a very smart and all understanding dog. He had long and clean pedigree. His breed was among the best in the dog family.

Everyone at home was extremely pleased with the new member of the family with such a strange name. At first, Tosha was also very happy. He was even inspired by a sudden change in his boring life. Amazingly, Tosha was not even jealous of the puppy. Even thought, most of the family attention turned mainly to a tiny and clumsy Break. The generous and already mature Tosha forgave everybody for everything. All this turmoil that the funny and fat puppy created, was exiting for him, as well.

In addition, the puppy Break was very kind by nature. He was constantly pleased with everything and everyone around him. Because of his excessive friendliness, the dog constantly wagged her tail. First Tosha, who was wised by his last summer vacation experience, perceived this dog gesture as a sign of aggression. It led him to some tension and his readiness to repel the attack. Only much later Tosha learned completely different dog language. They adapted to understand each other with the help of the master.

***

Cat and Dog

People say that some humans live "like a cat and a dog", referring to the implacable hostility between these breeds. It happens. But there are many cases with the opposite situations. For example, one old folk tale tells describes how a hunter lost a mitten in the winter. And then different animals found refuge in it. They, out of need, lived in peace and harmony, never quarreling.

Once the good girl Lila showed the drawing by E. Rachev to her cat Tosha and to the dog Break. She said: ". Look, how friendly you need to live!"

The friendship between Tosha and Break was created from their early childhood. At the time when the two month old puppy came to the family, Tosha was almost two years old. From early childhood they lived in the same apartment together. It was important for the peace and happiness of all households to have friendship between all members of the family. In addition, like all children, the cat and the puppy watched their owners. They observed all who lived nearby, and adopted the characters of their owners. Seeing the kindness and love of people, smart pets did not want to conflict.

The main cause of the hostility between cats and dogs is the different body language. In St. Petersburg apartment attentive owners of cat Tosha and dog Break taught them to understand each other. Especially Lila tried hard to help her pets to be respectful to each other.

She told Tosha that their dog Break wagging tail means greeting. And she explained

to her dog, that if cat Tosha curved his back, it means that he is very angry. At such moments, it is better to leave him alone. The girl taught the puppy that in cats, wagging the tail means irritation, unlike in dogs. And from the balcony she showed a black cat, which stood there with a curved back, ready to fight.

And then Tosha added that cats can also bend their backs and rumble when they feel good and pleased, especially when someone strokes them. At such moments, Tosha approached his main owner, the artist Valery, rubbed his foot, expressing that it was the time to cares him.

So, living together from an early age, the cat Tosha and the dog Break learned to talk to each other. And then they began to be very good friends and adapt to each other's body language. After all, people also learn not only foreign languages of other countries, but also the foreign language of animals.

***

Cleanliness

Cat Tosha had an obsession with the cleanliness. He expected that the girl Lila will teach the dog Break some good manners. Tosha meant that the dog should learn also how

to use the comfortable "human" toilet. But in the first days of his stay in the apartment, the puppy Break did all his "necessities" right on the floor. Soon Tosha noticed that the dog was creating too much new work for everybody, including himself. The owner of the house, the artist Valery, did not have the time to run out with the puppy from the fourth floor to the street for all dogs' natural affairs. So where this "necessity" found the puppy, there he did it all – on the floor. And the clean-up Tosha walked behind the puppy and tried to immediately clean and bury everything. But nothing disappeared. So, Tosha run to Lila and asked her to remove it right away. After several days of unsuccessful struggle for cleanliness, Tosha was exhausted and defeated. He could not even stand on his feet from fatigue, and he began to have an allergy. Tosha simply stopped moving on the floor, it was already above his dignity. He started jumping from cabinet to cabinet. And then he found a warm place on the washing machine. There, height up, he was waiting when the difficult time of the dog adaptation to the cleanliness would be finished.

Respect

Soon, Tosha began to notice more and more that his family was paying special attention to the little puppy. Moreover, they all forgive him for everything he did. At that time, cat Tosha decided to emphasize his superiority. He felt that he must to emphasize that in this apartment, he is the "navel of the earth." Tosha considered a puppy of Break was his ward. The cat Tosha began to walk around with his tail lifted. He was expressing confidence and firmness of his character with all its appearance. It did not make much effect on the kind Break, who already accepted Tosha as he was, with all narcissism and pride.

Then, Tosha more and more often began to tell the naive puppy about his adventures in Gelendzhik with the local robber cats. Soon, Break was convinced that Tosha was the real hero. This was a very happy moment for Tosha. He wanted that puppy clearly understood his authority in the house.

But soon cat Tosha got more concern. The puppy also loved to eat, and especially he admired the fish. For a cat, it was his favorite and the most pleasant time. But the dog Break ate very fast, just swallowing everything at once. Tosha did not keep pace with the dog, and decided to establish the boundaries of the permissible. From day one, Tosha refused to get his food on the same plate with the dog. But no matter what, Lila tried to bring the cat and dog closer. She fed them at the same time, placing plates close in the corner of the kitchen. In the beginning, Lila even stood by their side and observed that everything was peaceful and pleasant. She prevented cat from hiss at little dog.

Dog Break quickly and carefully licked and cleaned the bottom of his bowl. After that, the puppy laid next to the cat's bowl, periodically licking his lips, and watched how cat was eating. He was squinting at the cat and whispered that the food is more important for the growing organism of the dog, than for the lazy slacker cat. But cat Tosha ate, turning his head slightly to the left, then to the right, and did not listen to the dog's grumbles.

Once Brake, seizing the moment and put his face in a cat's bowl. But cat Tosha was on his guard. After he gained an extensive experience in his vacation on the Black Sea, Tosha knew how to fend for himself. In response, he painfully grabbed the dog in the nose. The girl Lila stood nearby and immediately shamed Tosha. But the cat explained that this was just a small warning to an expensive, but still ungrateful family member. Unsuspecting puppy Break was simply stunned by such a rebuff. He never again touched the cat's bowl.

But sometimes Tosha run faster and came to his boll before the dog. After eating all he had, he would hide the rest of the fish behind his back. Then he sat as if he did not know anything. But at the same time Tosha watched whether the dog Break would look for a fish behind him. For cat Tosha, the main thing was to show the young ignoramus that it was impossible to touch somebody else things. Seeing that the noble dog did not touch his fish without his permission, satisfied cat laid down in the middle of the room. Then, he started to teach Break to be more restrained in the food consumption. By this time Tosha himself already looked like a round ball, but considered himself moderately fit.

Before going to his bed, cat Tosha repeated some words: "If you are fat and clumsy, take at least some elegant poses. This golden rule is known even to cats."

Due to a not very active and not very eventful life, and also because of the cold Russian climate, the cat and the dog were always very hungry. They tried to beg for food, or get it wherever they could, even sometimes used illegal way.

One day, there were some butter, cheese, sausage and other wonderful delicacies were stored in the refrigerator. Cat Tosha convinced the dog that it is all right to open the door without the permission of the adults and get it all for a dinner. Naive and hungry Break firmly believed in the wisdom and superiority of the cat. Break was easily succumbed to his manipulations.

One day, when no one was home, Break opened this seductive refrigerator. The dog could not resist the seductive smell which was coming from that white big thing - refrigerator. They both fast ate the monthly supply of food. Then the dog Break remembered that he was forbidden to even come close to this white box with the delicious smell. But the arguments of the cat, who promised to take all the blame on himself, quickly convinced the dog's stomach grumbling from the hunger.

Later in the evening, Break felt completely out of place. His stomach was swollen and he fell ill. In fear, the dog hid under the desk and fell asleep. When everyone returned from work, he did not rush to meet the hosts, as usual. He did not lean out from there even at their cheerful call. He felt deeply guilty and could not tell that the cat was to blame. Then he finally came out, tail down under his legs, looking somewhere to the side. But his masters quickly forgave him, although they remained hungry themselves for a long time.

***

Games

Despite their age, everyone in the house loved to play some games. It was especially good to do after the dinner on weekends. They all enjoyed playing mostly hide and seek and catch-up. Everyone was hiding, and dog Break was looking. He quickly found everyone in small three-room bedroom apartment. At first, Break did not understand the game well, but learn fast. Then, he was carried away by the game. He especially loved when somebody threw his small ball into the back room. He ran there, found a toy, brought it, and waited to be treated with something good.

Joint games brought together all members of the family, both people and animals. Games brought great pleasure to everyone. After these hectic runs around the apartment, soon everyone calmed down, realizing that it was time for everyone to do their own thing. And then they all cleaned and went to sleep.

In mother Alena's apartment of St. Petersburg was rare, but peaceful cat-dog world. All family members, mistress Alena, artist Valery, girl Lila, Tosha and Break tried to do everything together and played a lot. Soon, the cat and the dog began to greet each other with their noses, and increasingly sleep in an embrace. The main thing was to pay equal attention to everybody. Because where there is no equality, there can be no friendship.

Only Tosha had his own idea of what the friendship of a dog and a cat means. He did not forget to remind Break that the cats belong to St. Petersburg Lion family, and generally divine family. Although Break was growing every day, he was still a very young puppy. One day when he arrived to this house, he found the cat already living there as a dominant leader. Then, cat Tosha taught Break that he was a hero at the Black Sea fight. So, Break believed in it, too. Dog Break loved Tosha under any circumstances. On whatever cat Tosha said to him, noble dog just replied that he was simply an ordinary German shepherd, whose role is to serve his people.

But Break had one, but the most important advantage, which Tosha greatly appreciated. A loyal dog walked with the owner, artist Valery, outside the house. But Tosha could not persuade anyone to let him go for a walk on the street.

***

Winter

So the first winter for Break came with its frosts and snowstorm. His owner Valery had to take the dog out twice a day. Especially Break loved morning walks with Valery. The dog felt good and confident next to his adored owner. If Break walked with girl Lila or with mistress Alena, but suddenly saw his master on the street, then his joy knew no bounds. It was hard to keep him on the leash. Dog Break was very strong. He could drug anybody a few meters on the snow. Then, Break would reach his master Valery and would be happy. Then he jumped on his chest and licked him happily.

More than anything, Break loved their walks in the wasteland. At six o clock in the morning other dog's comrades appeared in muzzles and on leashes there. Break, cheerfully, with a loud bark, ran after them through snowdrifts and mud. Even though Break was young, he was already huge and courageous dog. He did not find anything dangerous for himself outside the house.

And when Brake returned from a street walk, cat Tosha joyfully ran to him. The  cat carefully sniffed the dog from head to toe, studying what interesting Brake brought with him, in addition to the fleas. Tosha longed to know all the news that was outside, in a dangerous and difficult world for him. This was the world of fears and surprises about which Tosha had known some time ago. He learned about it in his vacation journey to the south. Only sometimes, before going to bed, Tosha spoke about his adventures on the Black Sea to the faithful friend Break. And they fell asleep, embracing under this strange tale.

But first, after any walk, Break was accustomed to be washed. When he returned from his  walk outside, he rushed into the bathroom and jumped into the bath. The bathroom was immediately covered with the dirt from the top to the bottom. And Break was waiting for his master Valery to wash him thoroughly. Then, the dog jumped out just as quickly from there, briskly shook himself, dousing everything around. Then, he also rushed cheerfully into the kitchen, sliding on the floor, and wanting to quickly see what was prepared for his dinner there. And Valery had to clean that human bath after his beloved dog.

Break always finished his dinner very quickly, although a cat hissed around him. But Brake did not pay attention at all to this hissing. After all these exciting joys on the street, he lay on the bedding under the master's table and slept immediately.

***

Tosha's Hobby

One day Tosha started a new hobby and followed this for a long time. Trying to  show Break that cleanliness in the house is his main priority, Tosha tried to clean the dog with his little tongue. When Break came from a walk, Tosha jumped onto the dog's huge head. He clung tightly to Break's skin so that the dog would not run away. Tosha licked huge face of the dog, trying to make him perfectly clean. But he did not have enough saliva for the huge face of the dog. This face was already almost the same size as the size of the cat. In addition, Tosha quickly got tired, and he also needed to wash himself afterwards.

All these new worries and problems really angered Tosh. Therefore, unable to cope with the incredibly time-consuming task of washing the dog's face, Tosha bit his nose slightly. It was indicating that it would be better for the dog to wash himself. But Break was not only extremely kind, but also a patient dog. He thought it was some kind of special game or a tradition of his new home. The dog patiently endured all the washes done by the cat with inevitability.

The lessons that Tosha cat gave about the cleanliness did not go in vain. After all of Tosha's effort, having endured all the cat's procedures, Break carefully took Tosha's small head into his huge mouth and licked it gently, playing with him.

Although Tosha was very tiny compared to the dog, he was older and wiser than the puppy. And indeed, life under one roof for all intelligent beings should have been as pleasant and comfortable as possible. The main thing in a good relationship is the ability to give in to each other and adapt to the habits of others. Animals understood this well and never quarreled.

***

Be useful

When the puppy Break appeared in the house, Tosha decided that the dog should be useful for something. When the winter came, Tosha started a new tradition. Once after

the dinner, Tosha jumped on the dog back and stayed there to be warm. Break did not mind. So they spent many nights together. Sometimes the cat wanted to emphasize again that he was the master in the house. So, Tosha came to the room, where the dog slept, and laid down on the dog special mattress under the table. Most likely, Tosha was simply pretending to be sleeping. Tosha stealthily

glanced at the dog, slightly opening one eye. Then, the dog would come to his place under the table, saw that the impudent Tosha already "sweetly sleeping." In the dog's sincerity,

Break did not have the strength to disturb his friend cat. He modestly squeezed himself closer to him, barely fitting in the same small mattress.

In winter, in the apartment was quite cold. Most often, Tosha slept between the master's bed and barely warm central heating battery. But the cat did not allow the dog to approach this pleasant place. Sometimes at night cat Tosha even moved to his master's feet. And over time, the cat began to move very closer to Valery's head. Tosha felt great there, like in paradise. He purred quite loudly as he tried to sing nightly lullabies for Valery. While feeling his master head, Tosha felt so good, that he began to snore. This did not bother Valery, and even amused, creating additional warmth and comfort. They snore happily together in unison.

Despite the effort of the masters to equalize the puppy in the same rights with the cat, Tosha always felt his privileged position and took advantage of this. And the good-natured dog easily accepted and recognized his authority. Sometimes Break had hard time with the cat. But most of the time, he understood that the happy life in a small apartment is important for all. So the cat and the dog were friends, despite their incredibly contradictory characters. They disproved the proverb about the opposing sides of these creatures by their peaceful lives. And the old sentence of "living like a cat and a dog" did not sparkle with truth at all.

***

Family vacation

Once before the family trip to the south, dog Break got very sick. Every year all necessary vaccinations were done for the dog and for the cat. But the dog was every day out playing with other dogs, and once he got a very serious canine "plague." Nobody expected this at all. Trying to save the beloved dog and cure this serious illness, the girl Lila began to give him the prescribed injections.

At that time in Russia there were no "one-time" syringes. Every four hours, Lila boiled the syringes in the kitchen, and injected the dog with medicine. This treatment was supposed to last for several months. And the family has long bought tickets to the south vacation. It was impossible to postpone this long-awaited trip to Gelendzik. So, the family collected their luggage and took a train to South.

On the train, loving his dog, Valery spent all days and nights in the vestibule with still sick Break. And Lila four times a day was continuing to give dog all necessary injections.

Break understood that they were trying to help him, and courageously endured all the suffering. He dutifully and silently tolerated everything that the good girl Lila did to him. Dog's love for his master was his strongest feeling. The dog does not know love for himself.

***

Vacation

This time the whole family came to Gelendzik again to the good grandmother Anna. But this time - already with a cat and a dog. Kind grandmother gave them again the same distant room with a terrace and a separate entrance to the courtyard.

At that time all stores in Gelendzhik was quite empty, as well as throughout the country. There was enough fish for everyone on the coast of the Black Sea. Therefore, for the whole vacation, the main food for the whole family was the cheapest fish called capelin and hake.

And this time, the cat Tosha several times dared to run away for the night and useless dates. The dog got used to serving and helping everyone. Therefore,

knowing that, Tosha told Break that he planned to go away for a new nightly adventure. Tosha hoped that Break would protect him, as well. But remembering the cat's tales of the past adventures with a local gang of cats, Break followed Tosha and quickly brought him back. Then still weak dog slightly scolded Tosha, reminding him of the danger of walking alone.

Instead of escorting Tosha through the challenging neighborhood, still weak from the illness, Brake loudly barked throughout the whole district. And all night he was echoed by many other local dogs. Their barks did not inferior him in the volume and bitterness. And now, in addition to the nightly yelling of the local cats, Alena, Lila and Valery could not fall asleep from the dog noise and excitements. Tosha was listening to the nightly dog's concerts on the terrace. Then, he sweetly fell asleep in the morning. He dreamed that when he would return to St. Petersburg, he could tell about his new trip to his friends. But he decided to tell about it from the top of his safe balcony. He anticipated the surprise of all the aristocrats of St. Petersburg and their enthusiasm for his southern adventures. It was especially important for Tosha that now he had a witness of his nocturnal adventures. It was his friend Break.

***

Dog School

Returning to St. Petersburg, the mistress Alena decided that their dog should fulfill its mission. He must serve and guard the apartment. Therefore, for this special training, it was decided to send Break to study at a dog school.

Tosha immediately felt that Break had received new special privilege. Tosha never wanted to stay home alone as before, and asked to take him with the dog under the supervision of the girl Lila and the artist Valera.

When they would return from the classes, Tosha scold Brake for some miscalculations and read him instructions on how and what to do next time in school. Patient Break took everything peacefully, remembering that Tosha had more experience in everyday affairs.

Finally, one spring, the artist Valery and the girl Lila put Tosha in a huge basket and took him to a dog school. There, all Shepherds stayed in a row and began to conduct their exam for the attention.

It was here that Tosha had to show that he was a real hero, and indeed could be useful. He was very glad that he could do something important for everyone and demonstrate his confidence. He was released on the walk in front of the long line of dogs. A brave cat walked slowly past the huge dogs. Tosha raised his tail as a pipe for the greater impression.

A line of shepherd dogs, including Break, was supposed to sit quietly, not expressing any reaction to their natural antipode. But still, some of them, especially emotional students, alarmingly and reservedly growled and grimaced. And others decided to just look the other way, and not to try to attack the cat. Only Break, accustomed to all sorts of Tosha's tricks, just yawned with the boredom.

After several months, Break graduated from the dog's school with the honors. Then, he began to receive the first prizes at many competitions, where the girl Lila took him to. And soon his whole dog's chest sparkled with all sorts of rewards.

Dog Break was very talented, but he was too kind to be a guard. Although he had a natural terrifying appearance, but in fact, he could not be taught or aggressive. So the master's dream of a dog guarding of the apartment was not destined to come true.

In any case, the artist Valera, mistress Alena and the girl Lila loved their pets. Break was an equal member of the family. But to everything else, he was still like a child for the artist Valery. The main goal of the mistress Alena (to make everyone busy) was successful, and everyone was happy. But life continued to wind up its natural circles and twists.

***

Circumstances

Suddenly, once, out of nowhere, "perestroika" came to Russia. The different new reforms began. It was beginning of the new and unusual way of life, to which people were not accustomed. Suddenly all was rolled downhill. Many enterprises began to close, large and seemingly unshakable organizations disappeared, as if they had never been. Many people lost their jobs. A vast country that existed for seventy years, the Soviet Union disappeared into one-part. Many people in Russia have lost themselves under the new conditions of breaking old foundations. They did not know how to live on and perceived social change with bitterness.

Mother Alena spun "like a squirrel in a wheel", working with tourists in different cities. She had to help, raise and educate her daughter Lila. Mother Alena was the one who always supported the whole family.

The artist Valery did not have a stable work, had nothing to live on. One day he left St. Petersburg forever. He took his cat Tosha with him to his motherland, to his mother's house in Ukraine. There he painted the walls of the cathedral, created icons and new paintings.

The cat Tosha lived happily for another eighteen years. Valery left his dog Break with his friends in St. Petersburg and did not give his address to mother Alena. The absolute devotion and love of the dog Break to his absent owner resulted in a strong longing and a broken heart. Soon, dog Break went to the other world.

In several years, mother Alena and her daughter Lila went overseas for a new life. And only twenty-five years later, on the Internet, they found the already famous artist Valery Bulat. Valery wrote to them about how the cat Tosha left him forever and went to the other world. Valery wrote:

"The last three months before leaving me for the other world, Tosha almost could not walk. But he tried very hard. Once, his back legs completely failed. Shortly before his final departure, he climbed under the closet. It looked like he felt something, and wanted to hide from it.

I carefully pulled him out from under the closet and laid him on the sofa. Then I lay down next to my cat Tosha. I put my palm under his head. Tosha was breathing heavily and looked at me with very sad eyes. I spoke comforting words to him for a long time.

Suddenly, several beads of the huge bitter tears rolled from his eyes right into my palm.

He did not want to leave me, and quietly said to me: "Muurr. Thank you for everything. I love you forever."

It was 10:45 pm. My good, old friend Tosha left me forever. After some sorrow, I buried him not far from my house under an old cherry tree. Every time I go to my work in the morning, I send him greetings. I remember our happy times with him in our happy apartment in St. Petersburg. I remember all magical stories of all cats of that wonderful city on the Rive Neva. But life was going on..."

***

Tosha's Dream

Once Tosha saw a strange dream. In his amazing dream, Tosha told his master, the artist Valery, where all the cats fly away from the Earth life. This dream said that all people, as well as all cats and dogs, all belong to the same moon. And Tosha described:

"It seemed that I was running in a beautiful field and smell grass: I do not remember any pain, death was like one big smell. And then it smelled of honey and mint, I flew into the grass to the whole ears. And I decided that in the new life (ninth) I will be the same who I was before, only better.

This place was called Paradise. All doors were always open here. It was cat's paradise. All cats wandered across Paradise in search of a home. And I wanted to be in the favorite warm hands, which would smell as the hands of my beloved artist.

It was the sun (looked like the sun I remember from the Earth in the window and in the South trip. It looked like a fish on the dish.

We were all here as the common cats. It is always warm, clean and dry, no rain, no snowstorm here. At night some cats dreams of dogs, growls at them in the sleep, but not too much. I am dreaming that I am running again in the field. Is everyone free to choose? I'm just a cat, I don't know anything. "

Enjoy each day

The other time, cat Tosha came out onto the roof and saw the ghost of a huge cat from another life. This huge cat roamed the rooftops with a butterfly net. And strange birds flew past him, and some characters of St. Petersburg and some monuments flew by.

Cat Tosha sat there for a long time. Then he decided that all this is also just a dream, which will soon pass, and again everything will happen again. So you just have to live and enjoy every real day, everything that this day will bring.

***

Our pets

The most popular pets for many people are cats and dogs. They are the most intelligent, easy to raise, most comfortable for living with a person.

Animals are infinitely devoted to the house, become attached to the person and love him passionately. They try to please the owner as much as they can. They do not know the word "betrayal." In some good families, pets become family members. But it also happens that people forget that animals have their own feelings and simple thoughts. And when animals grow up, they can be thrown to the mercy of fate.

It is caring for pets bring up the best qualities in a person. And it's best to start doing this from the childhood. When a person treats animals carefully, with love and care, so most often he will relate to other people. How much time a person would give to a cat or dog, the same way he would behave in any relationship.

Cats always surprise people. If the cat gets lost, it can still overcome hundreds of kilometers, but return to its beloved home. People consider a cat as a comfort at home and protection from mice and adversities. Some say that cats reduce the risk of serious illness and even prolong life. The elders say that there are two ways to become happier and forget about adversity: music and cats.

You should not be shy to caress, take pictures of your pets, and share your joy with friends. This, scientists say, strengthens the nerves and helps to survive stress. It is proved: stroking cat reduces blood pressure. They like to warm themselves and instinctively try to settle in the warmest place. The live heat of a cat very effectively soothes pain and helps fight inflammation. In honor of the some cats, people put monuments around the world.

***

Author

The author of the trilogy is Elena Pankey. She has created many fascinating books in Russian and English. Books published in Europe and America.

Two oil paintings on canvas are here. The first one is the portrait of Elena Pankey (Bulat) with her beloved cat Tosha. The portrait was painted in 1983 by her ex-husband, Valery Bulat.

It was done in Leningrad (St. Petersburg), shortly after they got married. Some painting is stored in California in Elena's house. The second painting is an auto portrait of the artist, Valery Bulat with his beloved dog, Break. This painting is stored in the artist's house in Zaporozhe.

The book also contains slightly modified drawings by the artist Tatyana Rodionova. Theses drawings dedicated to the cats of St. Petersburg. All photos and art slightly changed and redone by Elena Bulat.

All rights reserved

The author is Elena Pankey (Bulat). All rights reserved. No part of this publication may be reproduced, reprinted, stored in a computer memory, or copied in any form or by any means, including photocopying, recording, or other electronic or mechanical methods, without the prior written permission of the publisher (Elena Pankey), unless cited in brief . The title of the book is published in the United States of America. The main category of the book is Pets. Another category is Sculpture. The first edition was done in 2020. No copyright infringement is intended. To obtain permission for any publication, write to the publisher "Caution: Permission Coordinator" at: www.TangoCaminito.com

No copyright infringement is intended.

www.ingramcontent.com/pod-product-compliance
Lightning Source LLC
Chambersburg PA
CBHW081759100526
44592CB00015B/2496